Family Play Date

How to Kickstart and Nurture Family Traditions

Pamela Worth
and Tracy Scandlyn

Copyright © 2013 TinyTreks
tinytreks.com
All rights reserved.

Cover photography: Karen Sutker
Interior artwork: Lara Levitan

ISBN: 0615720218
ISBN-13: 978-0615720210

DEDICATIONS

For my incredible husband, Ron, and our four children - Sam, Karly, Talia and Rebecca. Thanks for allowing me to be the crazy mom trying out all my silly and hopefully meaningful ideas with you over and over again. I am so grateful for your openness. I love you all forever and for always. The memory of my father, Seymour Brownstein, with his beautiful, booming voice reading his poetry throughout my childhood has always been one of my greatest inspirations.

Pamela Worth

For my four boys and their amazing dad! Ryan, Jordan, Adam, and Luke, this book is, simply, for you. You are my most favorite people in the whole wide world, my greatest teachers, my deepest joys, my heart and soul. Getting to be your mom is the best blessing of my life! If I lined up all the boys in the world and could only choose four, I'd choose you!!!

Tracy Scandlyn

> Someone's sitting in the shade today because someone planted a tree a long time ago.
>
> Warren Buffett

Contents

Introduction 1

Making Mundane Moments Count 5
Sock Mopping 6
Handy Wipe Heaven 7
Warm Laundry Alert 8
Sock Party 10
Prince Ali 11
Putting Laundry Away 12
Five More Things 13

Fun With Food 15
Surprise Shortcake Supper 16
Taco Tuesday 17
Martinelli's for a Special Weekly Dinner 18
Pancake Sunday 19
Upside-Down Dinner 20
Hot Cocoa with Grandma 21
Midnight Ice Cream 23
Dinner Co-op 24
Awesome Applesauce 25
Ethnic Night 26
Baking Bonanza 27
Ritual Sunday Brunch 28

What A Difference A Day Makes...........31
Tooth Brushing Song...........32
Pajama Thursday...........33
High-Low...........34
Daddy's Home...........35
Back Drawings...........37

Once In A Lifetime...........39
Ear-Piercing Ritual...........40
Bar/Bat Mitzvah Trip...........42
The Other Mother Party...........43
You Are Now a Woman...........44

The Seasons of Your Life...........47
First Day of Summer...........49
Homemade Doughnut Day...........52
Family Flag...........56
Winter Picnic...........57

So Glad You Were Born...........59
Birthday Wake-up...........60
Special Plate...........61
Draw the Birthday Boy/Girl...........62
Breakfast in Bed...........63
Choose Your Birthday Meal...........64
Let's Give Something Back...........65
Circle of Encouragement...........66
Sing-Along Night...........67

Do Unto Others 69
Garage Sale 70
Neighborhood Walk-a-thon 72
Closet Cleaning 73
MS Walk 74
Change for Change 75
Soup Kitchen 76
Earth Week 79

Introduction

As mothers of four children each, we have spent the last twenty years looking for engaging, meaningful, and affordable ways to connect with our sons and daughters. This can be particularly challenging during difficult economic times, but the rewards for doing so are priceless.

One challenge parents of our generation face is that our children are born into a society with a media-driven value system. We are committed to providing traditions for our families that are nature rather than media focused, relational versus "me" focused, and philanthropic instead of consumer focused. Psychologists, authors, and experts in child development feel strongly that traditions and rituals are necessary for the development of healthy families. We agree, and **Family Play Date: How to Kickstart and Nurture Family Traditions** shows you how to create them even in the midst of financial struggle.

Intentional effort to create relationship-building activities requires thought and planning. Mary Piper, author of *The Shelter of Each Other*, convincingly suggests, "One way to take back our families is through ceremonies and traditions." A sense of identity and a feeling of belonging are promoted by effective traditions. This book's practical, recipe-style format provides easy-to-implement and inexpensive ideas for families.

Co-authors Pamela Worth and Tracy Scandlyn have collaborated to develop these time-tested traditions. You'll learn how easy it is to jump-start fun new family experiences, whether you are on a budget, or have plenty of resources and want better ways to create happy family experiences and memories.

Pamela owns Tiny Treks (tinytreks.com), a nature exploration program for young children, is a parent educator and life coach, and travels the country giving seminars and lectures. Tracy is the Executive Director of The Let Them Hear Foundation (letthemhear.org), whose mission is to bring the miracle of hearing to children who are deaf and hard-of-hearing in the United States and around the world. Tracy has had her own interior design business for over twenty years.

Okay! Ready for some family fun?

Cleaning your house while your kids are still growing is like shoveling snow in a snowstorm.

Phyllis Diller

Making Mundane Moments Count

Sock Mopping

Mopping is never an easy task, especially with hardwood floors throughout the house. We designed "Mopping Mondays" to get our kids involved and have fun while they're at it!

Ingredients: Damp socks for each child, and dirty floors that allow damp mopping.

Directions: Put damp socks on each child's feet and let them "ice-skate" throughout the house. Be sure to throw those now black socks right into the laundry basket!

Variation: Put socks on hands and feet. This brings out the giggles in everyone!

Making Mundane Moments Count

Handy Wipe Heaven

The person who invented individual cleaning wipes is a genius in our minds! Many a cabinet, door jamb, and countertop has benefitted from this modern convenience. When we're busy with household chores, our little ones often want to help, and they can when given a cleaning wipe.

Ingredients: Any brand of cleaning wipe.

Instructions: Give your child a wipe for each hand. Show them the areas you'd like assistance with, stand back, and be amazed at how much pride they take in their "grown-up" cleaning assignment.

Making Mundane Moments Count

Warm Laundry Alert

Having four children means the laundry piles are never-ending! In an effort to enlist help putting the laundry away, we began this tradition as a "call to action."

Ingredients: Clean, dry, and warm laundry, fresh from the dryer.

Directions:
Begin calling "warm laundry alert" aloud as soon as you remove the clothes from the dryer. Have your children lie down on the couch and simply pile all of the dry clothes on top of them. Allow them to remain under the pile as long as they want, but stay nearby. When they've had enough fun under the heap and begin to leave, you can ask for help folding.

Making Mundane Moments Count

Ten-Minute Tidy

Often, when we notice toys all around the house, we want to scold: "Clean this up now." However, the teachers and sweet southern mommas in us want to make cleaning up fun. We give everyone a ten-minute warning before a ten-minute tidy.

Ingredients: Kids and a mess.

Directions: Have a big stop watch or another fun way for the kids to see how long and short ten minutes can be. We assist during the entire ten minutes, which helps everyone stay focused.

Making Mundane Moments Count

Sock Party

Does this sound familiar? At the end of the week, ten socks sit on top of the dryer, and none of them match. By the end of the month there are twenty-five. After about six months, an entire basket of unmatched socks looms in the laundry room.

Ingredients: Two or more children, and mismatched socks. (This will work for gloves or mittens, too.)

Directions: Gather the children, start a stopwatch, announce, "Whomever gets the most matches wins!" and toss the socks all over—right on top of the children is recommended. Children have to make as many matches they can in a designated period of time. If they ask what the winner gets, say "A pair of matched socks, of course!" If that doesn't work, consider a great big sock hug.

Variation: Believe it or not, we actually made this an activity at a birthday party. Although friends looked at us in disbelief, he kids at the party had a blast.

Making Mundane Moments Count

Prince Ali

When our children were very little, we were always looking for activities to entertain them. An all-time favorite is what we've called "Prince Ali," after the character that flies on a magic carpet in Disney's *Aladdin*.

Ingredients: Two strong adults, one child, and a sturdy blanket.

Instructions: Place the blanket on the floor and have the child lie on his or her back. Both parents securely grasp the corners of the blanket, lift the child up off of the floor, and swing it gently back and forth while singing a favorite family song. The kids think they are flying, mom and dad get a bicep workout, and the giggles are endless!

Making Mundane Moments Count

Putting Laundry Away

If you're like us, you wonder why you didn't know that doing laundry was a major part of parenting. While the "Magic Laundry Genie" may never appear, you can enlist your little helpers to help ease the burden of putting all the laundry away.

Ingredients: Folded, clean laundry.

Directions: Put all the laundry in piles on one bed. Assign each kid a pile to put away neatly, especially if it's their own clothing.

Making Mundane Moments Count

Five More Things

We get tired of cleaning, and our children grow weary of hearing us ask for their help. Sometimes the whole house doesn't need a thorough scouring; a quick pick-up will do the trick. Remind your children that if everyone pitches in and returns just five things to their rightful spots, twenty-five items can be tidied in under two minutes!

Ingredients: Helping hands, an upbeat song, and two minutes.

Directions: Put a favorite song on the iPod, blast the volume, and ask everyone to spend two minutes putting away five things they find around the house. Make it fun and not a chore!

Fun-sized Snickers? Who's this fun for? Not me. I need six or seven of these babies in a row to start having fun.

Jeff Carlin

Fun With Food

Surprise Shortcake Supper

Sometimes the same old spaghetti, tacos and meatloaf dinner gets boring for both the cook and the consumers. Nothing is more fun at the table than a surprise dessert dinner - especially on a hot, summer day.

Ingredients: One large trifle bowl or other clear serving-dish, strawberries, shortcake (we recommend Bisquick shortcake, but crumbled crackers, pie crust, or angel food cake will also do), lots of whipped cream, long spoons, and a festive attitude.

Instructions: Prepare the strawberry shortcake and place it in the middle of the dining table. Spoons at each place setting are the only utensil needed. Use your usual "Dinner's ready!" call to summon the diners. Watch as everyone is surprised and delighted to find dessert waiting for them; no green beans in sight!

Fun With Food

Taco Tuesday

Feeding our busy families is a daily necessity, whether we have two hours to prepare a gourmet meal, or two seconds to put cream cheese on a bagel. Although we enjoy cooking, caring for active children and managing all of their activities can sometimes squash our chef hats.

Ingredients:
Ground beef or turkey, Lawry's taco seasoning (we've tested many, and this is the best!), taco shells, grated cheese, a can of beans, chopped tomatoes, lettuce and onions, sour cream, and salsa.

Directions: Follow instructions on the seasoning packet to make the meat. Place all other ingredients in microwave-safe dishes (we prefer to use containers to store leftovers without more dishes). Arrange the containers on the table and let the kids assemble their own tacos. It's okay if they don't use every ingredient, but encourage them to try everything, even if it's just on the side.

Easy variation:
If you don't have the energy for this, there's no harm in succumbing to the occasional "Taco Bell Tuesday."

Easier variation:
If you have even less energy, eat at Taco Bell so you don't have to clean up.

Easiest variation:
Send your spouse to the Taco Bell drive-thru!

Fun With Food

Martinelli's for a Special Weekly Dinner

Having regular family dinners contributes to a child's feeling of safety and belonging. Choose an easy, simple way to make one dinner per week extra special. We often do just that by adding a sparkling cider, like Martinelli's, to the menu.

Ingredients: Martinelli's, or other brand of sparkling apple juice.

Directions: Pick a night of the week where everyone really makes an effort to come home on time. It doesn't have to be a religious celebration, but keep it the same night every week if possible, so the kids look forward to it.

Variation: Pick other parts of the special dinner to make traditions. You can bake your own bread, have the kids pick different things to bake each week, or use a tablecloth to set the table in a special way.

Fun With Food

Pancake Sunday

How do we get to stay in bed on Sundays and dodge making breakfast? By dedicating Sundays to pancakes, because everyone knows that Daddy/partner makes them best!

Ingredients: One happy partner ready for a weekly tradition, hungry kids, pancake mix or a great homemade recipe, and a stove.

Directions: Enjoy taking the morning off from cooking to have a great meal with your family—though they may be having so much fun making pancakes they still leave you the joy of cleaning up!

Fun With Food

Upside-Down Dinner

Maybe you didn't inherit the "loves to cook" gene. Or maybe you're always on the prowl for creative ways to entertain yourself in the kitchen while providing healthy meals. Why not try serving breakfast at dinner? We're not talking a quick bowl of fruit loops, but a complete meal consisting of fruits, veggies, and protein.

Ingredients: Eggs, cheese, vegetables, and Canadian bacon for omelets; wooden skewers and fruit for fruit kabobs; potatoes for hash browns; juice and milk.

Instructions:
Since the menu is simple, ask your kids to help prepare. They may especially love to make the fruit kabobs! Make it a truly "upside-down meal" by having everyone shower and put on their PJs before they eat.

Fun With Food

Hot Cocoa with Grandma

We all know it takes a village to raise a child, and implementing rituals for your child to share with adult friends and family members can enrich the lives of everyone involved. We had an eager grandma who loved a weekly hot cocoa outing with our child. They would have a "tea party" weekly, spending at least an hour in the local cafe sharing hot cocoa, talking, drawing and playing.

Ingredients: Any eager adult willing to do something on a regular basis with a child.

Directions: Pick any simple activity for an adult and child to share, and by week two it becomes a ritual. If weekly isn't possible, monthly or even yearly works, too!

Fun With Food

Rainbows on a Rainy Day

This is a fun and delicious way to teach the colors of the rainbow to little ones, but kids of all ages can help!

Ingredients: Red, orange, yellow, green, blue, and violet Jell-O; a deep dish (preferably see-through), and a lazy rainy day.

Instructions: Make Jell-O one layer at a time, allowing each layer to gel in between. While waiting, take a walk in the rain, make boats to float in the gutter, or simply enjoy a quiet day inside.

Fun With Food

Midnight Ice Cream

It's easy to fall into the rut of being simply "functional," rather than fun, in the lives of our children. Kids typically love surprises, so why not dazzle them with a little midnight goofiness?

Ingredients: Transportation, a little cash, and a love of surprise.

Instructions: Pretend the evening bedtime routine is proceeding as normal. But... once all the kiddos are tucked in, wait a few minutes before marching right back into their rooms and ordering them up at once! Whisk them away for a late-night ice cream cone, or to the grocery store for ice cream sundae makings. Everyone--parents included– must keep their PJs on for this extravaganza. The surprise factor, plus parents' willingness to be silly, makes this a frequently-requested treat!

Fun With Food

Dinner Co-op

Chances are you aren't the only parent on the block looking for ways to reduce dinner-time stress. Try coordinating with one or more families to alternate the cooking of a regular group dinner. This practice not only enriches family life, it strengthens community, and maybe even offers the chance to try dishes you would never make. You may have one very full night of cooking when it's your turn, but remember that many responsibility-free nights will follow!

Ingredients: Two or more enthusiastic families who live in the same neighborhood.

Directions: Coordinate a schedule that accommodates all the families nicely. For example, families with two parents who work full-time might choose Sunday nights. If possible, involve families of different ethnicities to enjoy a variety of cuisines. When it's your night off, take pleasure in a late-afternoon trip to the park with your kids. When they ask, "Mommy, can we stay a little longer?" revel in saying yes, knowing that a homemade dinner will be ready by six. (Note: If all else fails on your night, splurge and order in for all the families.)

Fun With Food

Awesome Applesauce

When our children were small and apples were too hard for them to chew, we began making homemade applesauce. It's simple, healthy, and kids of all ages can be involved.

Ingredients:

3 pounds apples
1/2 tsp. Cinnamon
1 tsp. nutmeg (optional)
1-1/2 cups water
1/4 to 1/2 tsp. salt
Lemon slices

1. Cut the apples into one-inch cubes. Core and peel, or keep the peels on for a healthier sauce. 2. Put all the ingredients into a pot and boil, stirring regularly. (The kids love to stir with a big wooden spoon.)
3. Reduce heat to low and cover the pot.
4. Simmer for about 20 minutes until the apples are soft. May need to add more water.

Now the fun part: Mash the apples with a potato masher. If you don't have one, let the pot cool and put in a sealed bag to smash. It's fun to do this with bare feet.

Additional crafty apple project:

Make a large drawing of a tree on butcher paper. Cut an apple in half, and let the children use it to print apples on the tree with paint.

Fun With Food

Ethnic Night

Even if you don't live in a diverse community, we all live in a diverse world. With a little research, you may discover wonderful ethnic neighborhoods just outside your door. Celebrating Ethnic Food Night once a month will expose your children to the multi-cultural richness of the world.

Ingredients: A variety of restaurants in one authentic ethnic neighborhood. If that isn't possible, find ethnic restaurants in your neighborhood, or recipes for ethnic meals to be prepared at home.

Directions: There are many ways to approach Ethnic Night. Don't give up, and remember, this tradition may take practice!

Put scraps of paper listing different ethnic foods in a large bowl. Once a month, a different child picks blindly from the bowl.

As a group, brainstorm a list of different countries, write them in a notebook, and each month choose from the list.

If your child is studying a particular country in school, visit a restaurant that serves that cuisine. Give your child the task of researching the restaurants.

For an extra thoughtful experience, write restaurant reviews after the meal, so everyone can give his or her feedback.

Warning: Although Ethnic Night can be exciting, the first visit to a completely different neighborhood may be a push for your kids, especially since they may have never heard of, let alone tasted, many of the foods. Acclimating to such new flavors and surroundings may take a few outings.

Fun With Food

Baking Bonanza

Ahhh, baking! The gathering of the family, the gooey dough we all lick off of the spoon, the wonderful smell of freshly-baked cookies. We love doing our baking on Sundays so the kids can have homemade cookies in their lunches all week long, (or at least one day). One of our favorite, most fool-proof recipes, Kiss Cookies, makes baking with the family extra simple.

Ingredients: Flour, butter, powdered sugar, unwrapped chocolate kisses.

Recipe for Kiss Cookies:

2 cups of flour
2 sticks of butter
1-3/4 cups powdered sugar
1 tbsp. vanilla
Unwrapped chocolate kisses
Finely chopped or ground nuts (optional)

Directions: Mix all the ingredients with hands. Wrap dough around the kiss. (The dough can be pretty thin around kiss to yield more cookies.)

Bake at 350 degrees for eight minutes on an ungreased cookie sheet.

Fun With Food

Ritual Sunday Brunch

After a busy week and an errand-filled Saturday, a planned Sunday outing can be just what the doctor ordered. Whether you go to church, Sunday school, or just sleep in, squeezing in two hours for brunch can help end the weekend on a relaxing note.

Ingredients: A list of nearby brunch spots.

Directions: Pick a restaurant and go! We like to let our children do the deciding. If you stick to it and try a new restaurant every week, after a year your family will have experienced 52 different restaurants and types of food!

Courage doesn't always roar. Sometimes it is the quiet voice at the end of the day, saying 'I will try again tomorrow.'

Mary Anne Rademacher

What A Difference A Day Makes

Tooth Brushing Song

How many times have you literally pinned down your toddler or preschooler to brush his or her teeth? Watch your power struggles vanish as you institute a tooth brushing song!

Ingredients: Toothbrush and toothpaste of the child's choosing (this will help empower the child and make him or her more excited to brush), and a song that your child likes and is easy for you to sing (or try our suggestion below).

Directions: Have the child help put toothpaste on the toothbrush. While brushing or helping to brush, sing this song to the tune of "Rain, Rain, Go Away."

"Germs, germs, go away. We don't want you here today. Up and down, round and round, brush all over (your child's name) tooth town!"

Warning: You may need a longer or shorter song depending on the child's temperament. And remember to keep your fingers out of their mouth; if they want to stop your singing, they may bite!

What A Difference A Day Makes

Pajama Thursday

Today's parents and children are often overscheduled and under-relaxed. We picked Thursday, but Pajama Day can be any day, or even just a chunk of time, where everyone's dedicated to nestling up in their PJs and having no plans. Pajama Thursday is an excellent antidote to our often tightly-wound lives!

Ingredients: Small children, pajamas and scheduled downtime.

Instructions: When everyone wakes up, shout "Pajama Thursday!" This doesn't mean you can't go outside for a walk; it means not rushing anywhere, not having any plans, and staying in your PJs throughout breakfast, lunch, and maybe even dinner!

Variations: For some families, setting one day each week is best, but it can also be at random. For example, if your kids are school age, four o'clock might be a good time to put on those PJs and chill out.

Disclaimer: You may like Pajama Thursday so much you revaluate your schedule and opt for more pajama days!

What A Difference A Day Makes

High-Low

If your typical family dinner conversation sometimes feels shallow, sparse or even non-existent, this simple game is a great way to deepen the conversation and learn more about each other's lives.

Ingredients: A table, listening ears, and open minds.

Directions: Go around the table and allow each person to share the "high" and "low" of their day. Encourage everyone to really consider what the most positive experience of their day was, and also something that may have not felt quite right. Remind your children to really pay attention, especially when it's not their turn.

Variations: It may be too much to try this every night, but we recommend picking one night a week when you usually eat together. Or you can play only when company comes over, or only on holidays, or even just once to test it out.

What A Difference A Day Makes

Daddy's Home

(This was written to welcome Daddy home, but the song and arrival can change for whoever walks in the door.)

It is hard to tell who was happier when "Daddy" came home from work when the kids were little – the kids or mom. The kids joy came from fresh energy, and my joy came from another person who had two hands and didn't whine.

You hear about dads who need down time after a busy day. There was even a book written about giving your husband "cave time" for an hour when he came home from work. Hmmm. We knew that logic was not for us, as the dads would probably be living in a cave today if they really checked out for an hour each night.

We appreciate what great and involved dads our kids do have and I made up a silly song when our oldest son, was a tiny baby. It lightened the mood when daddy came home and, most importantly, it made him feel great. He jumped right into the mix of things the minute he walked in the door. We still sing it often when dad arrives home.

Ingredients: A song about Daddy coming home. Ours goes like this: "Daddy's home, Daddy's home, Daddy's home. It's the best part of the day. Daddy's home, Daddy's home, Daddy's home, HURRAY! HURRAY! HURRAH! (You can make up your own version).

Directions: Let the kids sing loudly and jump into Daddy's arms. Mom is often the loudest and *collapses* into his arms!

What A Difference A Day Makes

Bedtime Ritual

Bedtime rituals give beautiful closure to the day, and allow time to bond with your child. Reading stories, giving back rubs, saying prayers, and singing special songs are some of our favorites.

Ingredients: Parents, children and time.

Directions: With each of our children, we developed a slightly different ritual.

For our oldest: We read two books. (We were firm on two books because we knew how quickly it could become ten books) We tucked him in and sang him three songs. "You Are My Sunshine," "I Love You a Bushel and a Peck," and his absolute favorite, "What Did Sammy Do Today?" We made up that song and it went like this: "What did Sammy do today? Do today? Do today? What did Sammy do today? Let's ask mom or dad." When he was an infant it was things like, "Sammy made a big poop today, poop today, and poop today. Sammy made a big poop today. That's what Sammy did." It made it fun for my husband and me, knowing Sammy just liked the singing.

What A Difference A Day Makes

Back Drawings

Everyone loves the feeling of a gentle touch on their backs. Back drawings combine the relaxing effects of massage with the fun of a game. Even teenagers love the gentle touch, and because it is a game, it's acceptable to them.

Ingredients: Two people and a little imagination.

Directions: If you children are very young, draw pictures and shapes on their backs and tell them what they are—this is especially welcome during nighttime snuggles. If they're old enough, add letters and play guessing games with the drawings. With older kids you can progress from simple to challenging words. Kids often like to take turns and may ask to draw a picture, shape or word on your back, too.

Warning: Back drawings are relaxing, educational, and feel so good you may extend the bedtime hour.

If you can DREAM it, you can DO it.

Walt Disney

Once In A Lifetime

Ear-Piercing Ritual

In some cultures, ear-piercing is a ritual that occurs at a young age. In most American families, however, there is no pre-determined age for ear-piercing. We recommend choosing an age that you feel is logical and appropriate for your daughter(s), and upholding the rule despite complaints or begging. Having a set age is especially helpful if you have more than one daughter—the same rule will apply to everyone.

Ingredients: The conviction that you picked an appropriate age, and the guts to stick to it. Even if you think your daughter(s) may be ready earlier, it's important to uphold your original stance.

Directions: When the day comes, make it special. Help her purchase a pair of earrings she chooses in advance. Go to a reputable ear-piercing store, and take lots of pictures.

Variations: Ear-piercing could be tied to another milestone in her life, like a Bat Mitzvah. Or, if you need a great incentive for an ongoing issue, this could be it. You may not set a time, just wait for the appropriate issue for ear piercing to be the incentive.

Once In A Lifetime

Recording the First and Last Days of School

If you're like us, you have very few photos of your own school-age years. Now more than ever, technology makes it simple to keep a recorded history of your children's lives.

Ingredients: A camera, and children who are young enough to not be humiliated by their parents photographing them at school.

Directions: Get the kids to school a bit early on the first day, arrange them next to the school sign, and snap a picture. They may want to hold up a sign with their name and grade, so you won't forget in a few years (or possibly a few months)! Do the same on the last day, and when you compare it to the first day photo, delight in seeing how much they've grown. The school name is neat to have in the pictures, especially if you move or switch schools.

Warning: Starting by about fourth grade, your children may moan when you ask them to do this. By middle school the humiliation is too much-- unless you can all sneak to school for a picture in the middle of the night!

Once In A Lifetime

Bar/Bat Mitzvah Trip

We are lucky enough to have a grandma who asked us what we wanted her to do for our child's Bar/Bat Mitzvah gift. For her oldest grandson in our cousin's family she had purchased a pinball machine. I talked to my sister-in-law and told her my idea of making things more meaningful if, in the future, grandma would take each child on a trip. It could be as simple as an overnight in another city or state, or something more elaborate. The tradition began.

Because we have four children, my mother-in-law decided to double up with two kids and take them on a five-day exploration of London. It was an opportunity they never would have had otherwise, and they got great bonding time with one sibling and their grandma. Because of the pairing, our two middle girls got lucky and were able to go on two trips!

Ingredients: An eager and loving adult (a special grandma, aunt, friend, etc.) who can afford to travel.

Directions: Gently share your idea with the generous, loving adult. Explain that it would be more meaningful to mark this transition in a child's life with an experience, rather than a gift.

Once In A Lifetime

The Other Mother Party

The invitation came from our close neighbor across the street. Please come to an "Other Mother Party" to celebrate our daughter turning 18 years old. "What is this," I wondered? The card read: "You have all been an important part of our daughter's life, and have helped to raise and parent her. I invite you to find a bead that, to you, represents our daughter, and please join us next Sunday to celebrate her 18th birthday. If you would like to write a paragraph and relate it to the bead, that would be wonderful."

"Wow, I'm really in California," I thought. This was so out of the box, but I loved it. This young woman was strong and interesting, and because of this invitation, I ended up writing a long piece about her strength and inner beauty. The party was an afternoon I will never forget, and together a group of "other mothers" made her the most beautiful beaded keepsake necklace with shared words of encouragement and wisdom with her.

Ingredients: An 18-year-old woman, loving women to surround and celebrate her.

Once In A Lifetime

You Are Now a Woman

A girl's first period is a very special yet sensitive time in her life. Taking your daughter out to buy a "You are now a woman" piece of jewelry can be a wonderful, personal way to celebrate this sign of maturity.

Ingredients: A young woman and her mother, both willing to mark the occasion.

Directions: It's best to keep the jewelry simple. Many girls are quite embarrassed by the situation and can find overly-exuberant or proud mothers annoying. But there's no harm in assuring your daughter that her first period is a beautiful milestone, and doesn't have to be a secret.

The Seasons of Your Life

> **Wherever you go, no matter what the weather, always bring your own sunshine.**
>
> Anthony J. D'Angelo

The Seasons of Your Life

The Seasons of Your Life

Mulch Day

Turning mulching into a party instead of chore can foster a love of gardening in your children. Being outside in the fresh air, inviting friends to help, and working together to accomplish a task has made this a favorite fall activity for our families.

Ingredients: Mulch, small wheelbarrows, and small shovels.

Instructions: Invite all the neighborhood kids over for Mulch Day. Set up a water station, if you're so inclined. Help your worker bees fill their wheelbarrows with mulch to transport. They'll feel so grown up, and will love climbing to the top of the pile and squishing their little hands in the warm mulch.

The Seasons of Your Life

First Day of Summer

The first day of summer begins a period of rest and fun. We've made it a point to begin summer by having no agenda— except for eating popsicles!

Ingredients: Popsicles (lots of them!) in all flavors.

Instructions: Begin the day by telling your children that it's the first day of summer, and there will be no limit on the number of popsicles they can eat throughout the day. Offer popsicles for breakfast, and watch the smiles spread across their faces. Better yet-- let them catch you eating a popsicle for breakfast too!

The Seasons of Your Life

Apple Picking

I used to look forward with incredible joy to my family- of-origin's yearly trip to the apple orchard. I remember my father at the wheel with my mother at his side, and my four older siblings and me piled in the back of the car. Days like this—with all the regular fighting and hassles put aside for a special family outing-- felt so right for me. We even stopped for hot apple cider and caramel apples on the way home. I remember all my friends, who seemed to have much more structured family activities on a daily basis, envied all of our Sunday rituals.

I wanted to adopt this ritual when my own family lived in California, but, despite the amazing fruit produced there, the one fruit the Midwest is better for is apples. This year we were in Chicago in the fall, and on a gorgeous day we all piled in the car for apple picking. It was as wonderful as I remembered. All of our children, ages 3-12, were thrilled to pick their own bag of apples.

With rides and entertainment, the orchard is a bit more upscale now, but we stuck to good old apple picking, and then enjoyed warm apple pie a la mode in the orchard restaurant.

Ingredients: A vehicle large enough to fit the whole family, and baskets (if they aren't provided by the orchard).

The Seasons of Your Life

Directions: Even if you have to drive over an hour to visit a family-friendly orchard, it's worth it. Just sit back, relax, and enjoy the car ride.

Disclaimer: Times have changed, because my kids looked at me like I was insane when I suggested they bring an apple to their teacher the next day.

The Seasons of Your Life

Homemade Doughnut Day

Nothing tastes better on the first cool fall day than homemade doughnuts. This tradition is so popular that even the neighborhood children will begin to ask when it's Doughnut Day!

Ingredients: Refrigerator biscuits from your local supermarket, powdered sugar, and frying oil.

Instructions: Heat the oil in a large skillet. While the oil is heating, punch holes in the individual roll dough pieces. Fry the pieces until golden brown. Stir together powdered sugar and a small amount of milk until you have a glaze consistency.

Drizzle glaze over the hot doughnuts and serve. The doughnuts will be eaten as fast as you can fry them!

The Seasons of Your Life

The Magic Pumpkin

Though we're the first to admit we love Halloween and all its sweet treats, the sheer excess of trick-or-treat candy our kids sometimes bring home can be overwhelming. The Magic Pumpkin helps alleviate the potential sugar overload while allowing the kids to enjoy the holiday.

Ingredients: Paper, pencil, a small gift of your child's choice, and Halloween candy.

Directions: The night before Halloween, ask your kids to dictate or write a few choices of what gift they would like from the Magic Pumpkin, a special pumpkin that visits people's homes on Halloween night. Instruct your children that if they leave out all their candy, the Magic Pumpkin will trade it for a present. (This may be extra exciting for Jewish children who never experience Santa Claus.)

The Seasons of Your Life

Warning: Remember, it's only candy they're giving up, not their entire toy closet. Keep the presents simple. And of course, this may not work for all children. One of our children would not even consider trading her coveted candy for a silly toy-- but it was worth a try!

> Dear Magic Pumpkin,
>
> Here is all of my candy besides the 28 pieces that I kept. Rebecca and I have chosen to join our candy together in return for one big present. We would greatly appreciate a dippin' dots maker. It can be found at toys r us. Thank you so much!
>
> Love, Talia

The Seasons of Your Life

Pumpkin Carving

Everyone loves the pumpkin patch! Together with our families, we drive to a local patch one week before Halloween. End each child picks out a pumpkin that he or she can carry by themselves to the car. (This works well when they're small, but becomes more expensive when the teenagers pick larger and larger specimens!) Consider ordering dinner in on carving night to allow plenty of time for all of the design phases.

Ingredients: Pumpkins, carving knife, scoopers, paper towels, drawing supplies and a colander.

Directions: Each child first draws a picture of what they imagine their Jack-O-Lantern will look like. Next, help the little ones with the initial carving.

Variations: Host a pumpkin-carving party and invite the neighborhood. If you've just moved, this is a great way to get to know your neighbors.

Warning: This is a huge mess if you truly let the kids create, but it's worth it!

The Seasons of Your Life

Family Flag

Family traditions will long be remembered by your children, and one of the most creative activities you can do together is to design a family crest or flag.

Ingredients: Butcher paper or fabric (if you're ambitious), and, and art supplies.

Instructions: Explain that a family crest or flag represents the family's values and/or favorite activities. Divide the area of your flag into one section per family member. Each person has the pleasure of designing his or her own area. Parents should allow for creativity and age-appropriate artwork. Remember, the object is not to complete a Windsor-worthy masterpiece. Rather, you're collaborating on a treasure the whole family will enjoy for years.

Variation: If your family enjoys this activity, design a new flag or crest each year. Your interests and activities will change as your children grow.

The Seasons of Your Life

Winter Picnic

Cold weather, rain and snow can make the winter last forever. A winter picnic is a fun, easy way to alleviate the doldrums while staying warm inside!

Ingredients: A big blanket, an indoor space large enough for the whole family to sit on the floor, and cute picnic baskets for your food.

Directions: Arrange the blanket and picnic baskets in the middle of your family room or basement. When you call everyone down for dinner, shout, "It's a winter picnic!" Eating on a blanket in the middle of winter adds a really fun, surprising element to the night.

Warning: Keep the food easy to clean-- no marinara sauce or goopy foods.

> My father gave me the greatest gift anyone could give another person, he believed in me.
>
> — Jim Valvano

So Glad You Were Born

Birthday Wake-up

Playing music to children has been stressed since the catalogs came out, suggesting use of a music stethoscope to place on your pregnant belly, preferably classical music.

My husband and I are more of the rock 'n' roll types, so we started a birthday wake-up tradition the year our oldest son, Sam, turned one. Sam called us from his crib and we both eagerly woke up, ready to greet our crawling one year old.

We went into the living room and blasted The Beatles' "Birthday" song off the *White Album*. We twirled and danced around the living room with Sam overjoyed and giggling through it all. We bought Sam his own CD of the *White Album* when he was five. It has become a family tradition for everyone's birthdays. Often it's the alarm that wakes us up on our special day. We often have to drag our adolescent Sam off the couch to participate in the ritual for his younger sisters, but we seem to still be able to get a smile on his face while we sing.

Ingredients: CD of The Beatles' *White Album* (It comes in a two CD pack, or download). The song is called "Birthday."

Directions: Play the music and crank up the volume. Hold your child close, twirl plenty and laugh often.

So Glad You Were Born

Special Plate

As you might have guessed, celebrating is huge in our households. While we've been known to create parties for just about everything, birthdays are an occasion to go all out. Try ringing in your next family birthday with a special family plate.

Ingredients: Choose a plate that stands out from the rest, is unusual in its design or color, and/or has some significance to the family.

Directions: Beginning with breakfast, use this special plate to serve the birthday boy or girl every meal of the day. Decorate their place setting in a way that is unique to that child.

So Glad You Were Born

Draw the Birthday Boy/Girl

This is a fun way to have a life-size memento of your child on his or her birthday.

Ingredients: Colored markers, a roll of craft paper, and plenty of family and friends.

Instructions: Have the birthday child lie on the floor atop the craft paper. Trace around the child's shape with a dark marker. After he or she gets up, have all family and friends present fill in the outline, portraying the birthday child's clothes, physical features, hair color, and anything else they can think of. Encourage everyone to express his or her artistic flair! When finished, carefully roll up the paper and store—you'll want to compare if you do it again next year!

So Glad You Were Born

Breakfast in Bed

In our homes, it's imperative that the birthday person sleeps in and receives a gourmet breakfast in bed—especially if that person is mom!

Ingredients: Food of the birthday person's choice.

Directions: Allow the kids to prepare, or help prepare, breakfast for the adult. When it's a child's birthday, involve the entire family in the process.

Warning: When the kids are little and you're trying to let mommy or daddy sleep in on their special day, it's tough to contain the excitement. When the kids are teens, it's hard to wait all day to wake them for breakfast!

So Glad You Were Born

Choose Your Birthday Meal

In this straightforward and popular tradition, the birthday person gets to choose the site of their special birthday dinner. Depending on finances, it can be a favorite homemade dinner or a favorite restaurant.

Warning: You may end up spending several birthdays in a row at your local Taco Bell. Thank goodness mom and dad can choose their favorites, too!

So Glad You Were Born

Let's Give Something Back

If you're reading this book, you probably have healthy food for every meal and more than enough toys, clothes and gadgets. This tradition will help your child learn that much of the joy of receiving is the joy of giving back.

Ingredients: A grateful family, and presents.

Directions: Once they receive all of their birthday presents and before they use them, encourage your children to choose an equal number of toys or clothes they already own to donate to charity.

Variation: Ask your child to donate just one of their gifts, especially if it's a duplicate. Some especially large-hearted children may consider asking for donations to a cause of their choice rather than receiving a gift of their own.

Warning: It's much harder for the little ones to part with their toys, even if they haven't looked at it in a year.

So Glad You Were Born

Circle of Encouragement

The saying goes that five encouragements are needed to balance every one criticism. There's no place like home for receiving words of appreciation and gratitude.

Ingredients: Fifteen minutes and enough chairs for everyone.

Directions: Select one family member to be the recipient of the gift of encouragement. Arrange a circle of chairs around the chosen person's seat. Take turns expressing thoughtful words about him or her.

So Glad You Were Born

Sing-Along Night

Is there a child or parent in your family who plays an instrument seriously, or even just dabbles? If so, a regular sing-along not only nurtures family togetherness, it gives your musician a chance to squeeze in a little extra practice!

Ingredients: A musical instrument, a person who can (even somewhat) play a musical instrument, and a good music book with songs the kids know.

Directions: Pick a night of the week that will mostly work in your house, gather the family 'round, and sing!

Variations: If no one can play an instrument, just sing.

Warnings: Older kids can much less enthusiastic (to put it nicely) than little ones. If this is the case with your family, remind them in advance that it's Sing-Along Night, and ask them to be pleasant.

> How wonderful it is that no one need wait a single moment to start to improve the world.
>
> Anne Frank

Do Unto Others

Garage Sale

Encourage your kids to have a charitable garage sale. It can motivate you to clean up, organize and eliminate old or unused stuff while simultaneously helping others. With a little goal-setting, your kids may beg to have a garage sale every year!

Ingredients: Gently used clothes and toys.

Directions: Set a goal to make enough money to purchase something someone else needs, or to make a significant donation to the charity of your choice. Choose a date and begin cleaning up a few weekends beforehand—this is a chance for the whole family to help each other.

Allow the kids to implement the plan from start to finish by creating signs, posters, banners, and flyers for the neighborhood. Price all items and work during the garage sale.

Do Unto Others

Carnival for a Cure

If your child or your child's friend or classmate has a serious medical condition, hosting a carnival to raise funds to support the cause can be fun and meaningful...

One of our oldest daughter's best friends had juvenile diabetes. Karly was in a big group of friends and she was the only one celebrating a Bat Mitzvah. We decided to create a Carnival to raise money for JDRF as her mitzvah project, which was mandatory in our family. We involved all nine of Karly's group to advertise, create and run the carnival. We raised over $1000.00 the first year. It has now become a tradition and our youngest daughter Rebecca now has a good friend with juvenile diabetes. We have included every girl in her grade that wants to participate and at last count we have 39 girls who will be involved in this year's carnival. I am retiring from running it and our 16 year old daughter, Talia has completely taken over the communications, meetings, etc.

Ingredients: A cause you believe in, eager children up for a challenge, advertising flyers, and a physical location.

Do Unto Others

Neighborhood Walk-a-thon

Each spring, our neighborhood council chooses a family in need of support due to illness, the birth of a baby, death of a loved one, aging, or other trying circumstances. As a group, we brainstorm ways to assist creatively. One year we raised money for an elderly neighbor's yard service by hosting a neighborhood walk-a-thon.

Ingredients: A neighborhood council or otherwise motivated group of neighbors, a family or individual in need, and creativity.

Instructions: Begin this thoughtful tradition by suggesting it at your next neighborhood council meeting. You may need to volunteer as chairperson of the event for the first year. After that, there will be others vying to lead as this becomes a neighborhood favorite.

Variations: Your group can host bake sales, walk- or dance-a-thons or babysitting co-ops – your creativity is your only limit.

Do Unto Others

Closet Cleaning

If philanthropic events and socials are common in your town, chances are your neighbors' closets are full of fancy ball gowns, cocktail dresses and holiday attire. Typically, these frocks are worn to one or two events, and then end up crowding the closets. Instead of taking up space in the dark ends of your wardrobe, why not put those garments to good use and host a closet cleaning for charity? One example is donating party dresses for high school students during prom and homecoming seasons.

Ingredients: Unused party attire, and a willingness to part with all that velvet and lace.

Instructions: Invite your friends and neighbors to gather and drop off their dress-up clothes to you on a specific date. Contact your local high school and arrange an evening of "free shopping" for the students. Gather your friends, and enjoy one of the best shopping experiences of your lifetime. Local stores may provide mannequins, hanging garment racks, and other store accessories you may need.

Do Unto Others

MS Walk

My sister-in-law has multiple sclerosis (MS). Modern research and incredible drugs have helped her stay healthy for the past ten years--but she is one of the lucky people. Every year we walk in the MS walk with her team, WORTH THE WALK. At first she was hesitant to ask friends and families to share this morning with her. But she overcame her fear, and since has done an amazing job writing a beautiful letter and organizing a fun group to walk every year. This has become a ten year family tradition, and even the teenagers don't complain about getting up early. We've even had a child or two in a cast doing the walk, limping along.

Directions: Find a cause or share someone else's, and make a yearly ritual around a bike ride, a walk, a run, a bowl-a-thon or a skate-a-thon. It's something the kids remember, and you're supporting a special person in your life.

Warning: Walks like these are typically held very early in the morning.

Do Unto Others

Change for Change

Maintaining a "Change for Change" jar in a centralized area of your home is a quick, easily-accessible way to raise money for donating. You may consider donating to various causes that come up at school, places of worship, or in your neighborhood. Regularly collecting for and donating to charity contributes to community-building, and fosters a sense of philanthropy in your children.

Directions: Break out the stickers, markers, ribbons, scraps of wrapping paper and tape, and have the family decorate a jar together. Consider getting others involved by hosting a Change for Change jar-decorating party, so that other families and friends can share in the tradition.

Warning: When in a rush, you may be tempted to dip into the jar for lunch money!

Do Unto Others

Soup Kitchen

We received a letter from our temple asking if anyone wanted to create a dinner and serve it at the Inspiration Cafe soup kitchen in Chicago. We signed up for a slot for a few months later and forgot about it. I received an e-mail a month before the date that explained we would shop, cook in the cafe kitchen and be waiters and waitresses to serve individuals and families dinner. The kids were told this was a non-negotiable family experience, and luckily our college son was in for spring break. Together we shopped for food and arrived at the Inspiration Cafe to cook and serve food to about 80 people.

A sweaty four hours later, we sat together as a family with some of the other workers and enjoyed the meal we had cooked together. The concept was that research showed if people who are struggling share a healthy meal together in a restaurant style setting, it may change their aspirations and desires in life.

Whether it's this model or simply a yearly visit to a soup kitchen, make sure your children experience all kinds of lifestyles. They will understand that everyone, no matter what their socio-economic status, is a human being who values interactions.

Do Unto Others

Ingredients: A sense of compassion.

Directions: There are many opportunities for families to have first hand experiences helping others.

Warning: One of our kids said after our first visit, "Can we do this every Sunday?"

Do Unto Others

Beach Clean-up

Earth Week or the first day of spring are perfect times to take the family to the beach for a post-winter clean-up.

Ingredients: Gloves, garbage bags.

Directions: Try setting a goal, like picking up enough cans to fill an entire garbage bag. You can go as a family, or join an organized clean-up group.

Do Unto Others

Earth Week

Be it Earth Day, Earth Week, Earth Month, or any time of year, try committing to one regular, family-oriented, eco-conscious activity. It could be as simple as walking to the store once a week instead of driving.

Warning: Follow-through can be hard, so choose goals that are realistic and achievable.

Here are more ideas:

One day a week, prepare a completely waste-free lunch.

Pick one park per week in which you and the kids pick up trash for ten minutes, and then play for ten minutes.

Buy no prepackaged, individual-serving-sized foods for a month.

Send everything for lunch in recyclable packaging.

Have a party with more than ten guests and do not use paper plates. (You'll be shocked by how easily your friends will bond while washing dishes together.)

Encourage your kids to pick up five pieces of garbage a day as they walk to school or walk the dog.

Do Unto Others

On the first day of spring, go to a local beach or lake and pick up trash.

Reuse items like toilet paper rolls and egg cartons for craft projects.

For more ideas go, visit the *For What It's Worth* blog at tinytreks.blogspot.com.

We hope you enjoy the ideas in **Family Play Date: How to Kickstart and Nurture Family Traditions.** There is nothing sweeter than holding your child close and laughing together. The focus on family fun, creating new traditions and cutting down on media and TV time brings its own rewards.

It is so important for all of humankind to stay connected with nature. Through wonderful hikes, music, crafts, snacks and stories, **Tiny Treks** families enjoy the natural world while staying connected to each other in the process. For information on programs with children, get in touch with Tiny Treks. Visit tinktreks.com and the *For What It's Worth* blog at tinytreks.blogspot.com.

A portion of the proceeds from **Tiny Treks** books goes to charitable causes that benefit the needs of children.

Made in the USA
Lexington, KY
27 January 2013